Credits:
>   Art Work: Isaac Canady
>   Cover Design & Layout: AquaScor Ventures

Contact Information:
blackrosecity@gmail.com
facebook.com/frederickdouglass.knowles
http://asv.aquascor-design.com/

BLACKROSECITY

Frederick-Douglass Knowles II

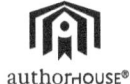

authorHOUSE®

AuthorHouse™
1663 Liberty Drive
Bloomington, IN 47403
www.authorhouse.com
Phone: 1-800-839-8640

First published by AuthorHouse 04/6/2011

ISBN: 978-1-4567-2953-0

Printed in the United States of America

Any people depicted in stock imagery provided by Thinkstock are models,
and such images are being used for illustrative purposes only.
Certain stock imagery © Thinkstock.

This book is printed on acid-free paper.

Acknowledgements

To *The Magnificent One*, for choosing me; Poetry, for keeping me up at night; Mommy (LaForest Knowles), for raising 11 kids; Gammy, for establishing the foundation (575); my siblings, for raising "Cabbage Head;" my daughters Lanaisha and A'meé, for shaping me into a man; Isaac Canady, for the impeccable, original artwork (you are truly gifted *daddy*—your time is now— and you said you're done with art!); Alain Lopez, for creating the forum *BlackRoseCity,* and tolerating my indecisive-Libra- ness during graphic designs for the flyer and MySpace page; Olusanya Bey, for spiritual insight and Catan conquests; Iyaba Ibo Mandingo, for guidance in this game "iron sharpens iron;" Leah "Lockedown" Prescott-Burgess, for the warrior wake-up call; Croilot Carlos Adames, for the late-night-over-the-phone- ciphers; Kerry McFarlane-Mallett, for being a long, lifetime (NFA) friend; Dr. Ken Florey, for believing in the poet that bum- rushed his office nearly 7 years ago; Jeff Mock for the countless revisions; Tameka "Inertia Justice" White, for the North-South beef battles; all my people's in the CT, national and international poetic circle (you know there are way too many of ya'll to list!), family 4life; to the entire *BlackRose*, all of my child and adulthood friends who helped etch these memories into black & white; and all of you who've lent me your ears, hearts and souls, thank you for encouraging me to achieve this milestone.

Luv, Light & Thunder…

Frederick-Douglass (Knowledge-Yesod) Knowles II

To my daughters: Lanaisha & A'meé

The optimist sees the rose and not its thorns;
the pessimist stares at the thorns, oblivious of the rose.
– Kahlil Gibran

Contents

How Many Fanatics In the Cosmic Realm of Roller Skating Actually Overdosed on Rhythm and Speed?

I laced my shiny black boots
and dashed to the boy's bathroom
to christen fluorescent
green "zingers" in lukewarm water.
That assured my wheels
an extra grip.

Disco lights flickered
like electronic Christmas trees.
Huge box speakers
dangled from the ceiling
blaring Michael Jackson's "Thriller:"
It's close to midnight . . .
Vincent Price hypnotizes
ambitious roller boogies
with *the funk of forty thousand years . . . .*

Saturday nights
belonged to the skate gods;
we, merely obedient zealots
circling their shrine.

Wilbur rolled in reverse,
sporting blue Dickies
and a crisp white polo T
embroidered *skate guard.*
He never benched anyone
for speeding.

Marshall owned the only pair
of triple jump-bar skates
ever seen in the *Rose*;

shiny, crisp blades
reflecting psychedelic hues
of turquoise, green and gold
that mesmerized white girls
as they floated past
waving blonde locks of allure.
Pete fancied an old wheel
for a toe stopper; cool,
the way he'd cut his ankles
screeching his plump frame
to a halt.

An exhilarated Chanise
offered me five dollars
for a blind couples' skate.
I did the math, two slices of pizza,
a coke and some chips for two songs . . .
deal.

Allison, the economically
advantaged out of the group
dished out her allowance
for Pole Position tournaments.
And I, I was the Shoot-the-Duck King,
the undefeated Chipped-Tooth-Champ.

When Afrikka Bambaata's
"Planet Rock" hit the turntable
we'd drop conspiracy theories
on who shot J.R.?
And wager how many laps
one of us could achieve
before Rolo,
the by-the-book guard,
blew his whistle.

We ignored his shrieks.
No time for rules.
Only time for speed.

More whistle-blowing
and then, Rolo's pointed finger,
his direct order to get off the floor
and sit by the office.
Damn! I got kicked off again!
eight laps into "White Lines,"
Melle Mel's prophetic hook shouting
to a skate feign on the verge of od'ing to
 don't don't don't don't don't don't do it
ba ba ba ba ba ba baby!

Too late.

During my 10 minute
suspension,
I contemplated
how many fanatics
in the cosmic realm of roller skating
actually overdosed on rhythm and speed
in a world of bliss and 80's pop music?

Times up.
I pressed my black toe stopper
firmly into the carpet,
assuring me a solid thrust
back onto the floor.

Ashes

On the side of our garage
we had a rosebush,
fairly tall, massive in width,
buds sprouting against
a chipped concrete surface,
prickles twining around a fence
shaped by Gammy's worn Georgian hands.

Those Southern hands labored
in a self-owned New England plot,
accustomed
to plucking tomatoes,
spraying collards,
planting marigolds
and shooing horseflies
while commanding
11 hardheaded grandchildren
to stop plucking sour grapes
and half-ripened pears
before she spanked our behinds.

Those chapped,
blood trickled hands
never cleansed
before wrenching worn life
from the base of that bush,
clipping old thorns,
snapping dead branches,
watering sun-beaten top soil.

Someone's pale hands
nailed a wooden cross to that bush,
doused its petals in kerosene,
and set it aflame.
Streams of fire-orange cinders

ascended past a backroom window
where Alex Haley's premiere
of *Roots* transmitted chattel
across a snow-filled black and white tube.

Flashbacks of a once
golden era of supremacy
must have driven those hands livid;
witnessing a sole negro family
reside in the biggest home
with the largest plot
overlooking the neighborhoods
of East Great Plain.
Those icy, cold palms
flushed with rage
as shrubs of burgundy flesh
flamed to the bellows
of "*Nigger, you besta go home,*"

flamed
like charred, burnt bodies
of young boys
dangling
from steel magnolias,

flamed
like opened
white meat wounds
smothered in salt,

flamed
like premature pubic thighs
after masta
done plunged
his manhood
into pink rivers
of blood and semen

sailing southbound
to the Mississippi,

flamed
like the hearts
of 11 grandchildren,
who stomped those hands
like the ashes of a burning bush
crushing any last hopes
of a neo-dixie revolution
sparked
by the descendants
of pseudo-abolitionist
bastards
mad cuz America done let these
porch monkeys
take over the big (white) house,
planting sustenance --fuck cotton

--America ain't let nobody take nothing
especially suttin' they done took.

The joints of those worn Georgian hands
swelled endlessly day and night
so that 11 hardheaded grandchildren
could pluck sour grapes
and eat half-ripened pears
without someone wrapping
a noose around their necks
or sailing
pirated vessels into pink rivers.

A declaration of our conviction
caused those white boys
to approach with nothing
but respect;
throwing up sweaty palms,

offering truce;
swallowing truth
that these big, (white) house *monkeys*
ain't going nowhere
triggering
their icy, cold palms
to tremble in fear
every time they passed
that rosebush
on the side of our garage.

FINAL FRONTIER

Kindergarten class was my final frontier.
Its sun splattered walls housed
a color blind utopia of children
who resembled each complexion
under the milky way. Almond-White,
Cinnamon-Brown and Golden-Yellow
spectrums of light
formed a uni-race of a rainbow,
on the other side of Ms. Fitzgerald's
classroom door.
Her warm smile and frosty white hair
welcomed her students at the entrance.

We began class with basic math,
 reciting numbers, counting all the way
up to twenty-five, our goal for the week.
Storytime solved the mysteries
of why whales spit water
out the hole on top of their head
and how kangaroos bounced up and down
never dropping their babies.

During playtime
I tied on the little white apron,
nuzzled the fitted cap
and sold goods from the corner store,
exchanging paper coins
for empty cereal boxes,
thanking my customers
for their service.

Tuesday afternoons was sing-a-long.
Amy's dad, Mr. Jeffers,
scooted underneath the doorway,
guitar case slung over his back.

We gathered in a semi-circle,
sat Indian style and sang to his melodic strum,

Bluebird, bluebird in and out my window,
Bluebird, bluebird in and out my window,
Bluebird, bluebird in and out my window . . .

The funny knot in his throat
slid up and down to the chorus,
Ooooh, Johnny, I'm tired . . . .

I never grew tired of the Bluebirds,
but the *other* side of Ms. Fitzgerald's
classroom door
didn't believe in rainbows.
It didn't believe cinnamon was brown
or yellow was golden,
or that Blackbirds should fly
amongst Doves.

Natural Born

asians
wanna be europeans,
europeans
wanna be africans,
and africans just wanna be free.

hispanics
are called latinos;
latinos
don't like gringos
and gringo's nearly a euphemism
for lightly tinted negro.

now the cape verdians
despise the portuguese
and the portuguese diss cape verde,
but since they're both located
off the coast of Africa,
you tell me?

if you speak with a greek
on the philosophies of socrates
what would you do if you knew
zeus descended from Timbuktu?

sicilians
are really north African civilians
exiled by the millions
when the Pharaohs
revoked their hospitality
and tried to kill'em.

-while the chinese
are the ones
connected to the huns,

while the kara khitai
(black mongols)
stomped out of persia
desecrating asia under the sun.

mexicans
are really light-skinned
Nubian brethrens
host of the Olmec statues,
before their lands
became commercial.

eskimos
the frozen negroes
year after year
escorted vikings
to the western frontier.
and i'm really amused
with the jews
since they bounced
out of Ethiopia
and got confused
cuz they believe judaism
started out white
and shun the birthplace
of humanity out of spite.

the men of india
like to pretend to be Godsend
but culturally enslave
beautiful Bonda women.

so what's really going on?
alpha to omega Africa
will remain strong.
deceivers will lie,
claiming text books aren't wrong,

but whether you're
latin-asian-indo-european
you're still natural born.

THE PRISON INDUSTRIAL (COMPLEX) SLAVE SHIP
(prisonactvist.org/prisonlabor/sources)

It sets sail
when Americans
take flights on TWA
and touch ground
in Anytown, USA
eager to devour small fries and Big Macs,
surfing the internet on their Compaq
oblivious to the power
of their consumerist acts.

The anchor is cast
when Texas Instrument,
instruments devices to ensure
no child (is) left behind,
reporting an increase in profits
while their father is doing hard time.

In the world
of information technology, ironically,
Dell doesn't disclose that their laptops
are manufactured in penal colonies.
Foundations are constructed
with the molding of Kaiser Steel
while the family structure is torn apart
as a result of their deals.
Like the bottom of a ship
lingered in the stench of doom
prison industrial slaves
build Microsoft Windows
in windowless rooms.

(Queen) Victoria's Secret
has finally been revealed.
How generations after her reign, her name

is still linked to the slave assembly wheel.
Even Pierre Cardin's hand
is deep in on the peonage plan.

Do you ever stop and wonder why,
inmates have to call home collect
even though they're contracted to MCI?

And 3Com,
who's business partners
run the State Pen.
Les we forget IBM,
who funds consultants
to track the failure
of fourth grade boys
predicting their future
as Incarcerated Black Men.

It sets sail
whenever we flip open Motorolas
pressing send, when our children
canvass the shelves of Toys R' US
for barbie and ken.
AT&T will disconnect you
if the bill is past due,
even though members
of the chain gang
only receive a fraction
of the revenue.

It's tragic how a mulatto (Halle Berry)
might not actually know,
that her Revlon Colors campaign,
was bored off the backs
of the disenfranchised
who recite numbers
instead of their name.

Hour after hour
they slave labor for Eddie Bauer,
with Boeing & Honeywell
sucking up the sap.
And Nordstrom made a pact,
if blacks get locked up for crack
they ain't paying us jack.

Jostens & Nortel
will most likely never tell
that their bucket is dipped
in the bottomless black well.
Kodak and Adobe
capture timeless moments
developed in print shop,
but the picture of freedom is blurred
whenever that slave ship
approaches their dock.

The Constitution claims
separation between church and state,
but the mere pews we sit upon
every Sunday morning
are being made upstate.
Praise the Lord.
Pass the collection plate.

The 13th Amendment made it legal
to enslave and exploit
brown and black people:

> *. . . neither slavery nor involuntary servitude*
> *except as a punishment for crime*
> *whereof the party shall be dually convicted*
> *shall exist within the united states*
> *or anyplace subject to their jurisdiction . . . .*

It sets sail
whenever Americans
swipe that magnetic strip,
when we stuff our bellies
and plan exotic trips
oblivious to the facts
that our consumerist acts
contribute to the slashing of backs
on the prison industrial slave ship.

Recipe

(Cookbook: How to Make a Negro Slave)

frozen son --diasporic offspring
armor --stripped
independent psychological state --still
ten dollar tax --bartered: brass, tobacco, guns, rum, iron, copper
1712, evolution, cross to noose --300 years guaranteed
breastfed --fear, envy, distrust
pitted old --against young
light --against dark
King --against Queen
taught love, trust, respect --out of fear
lab specimen --reduced natural state
subhuman --independence broken
economic cardinal principle:
break nigger --like horse
bound, tortured stud --tarred, feathered
psychologically contained --*keep the body…take the mind*
soul snatched -- goal, long range
female, child, focal --future generations
mother --*extract… last bit of bitch out of her*
offer son --reverse nature
frozen fear --sound sleep economics
infant slave process --orbiting cycle
Queen re-shifted --King exiled
companion frozen --victimized, negotiated
historically detached --familial severed
mother tongue --annihilated
alien language --instituted
basic ingredient --fool
chef (author)--william lynch

Five Chiefs

By the end of the millennium five men controlled the world's media.
And the people rejoiced, because their TVs told them to.
-- Michael Moore

4 major companies--
National, American, Columbia
and Mutual Broadcasting Systems--
own 95 percent
of the radio waves.

9 major companies--
Time Warner, Disney, Bertelsmann,
Viacom, News Corporation, Sony,
 TCI, Universal, and NBC--
own 98 percent of the airwaves,
dictating 98 percent of global advertising.

the FCC
issues licenses
entitling corporations
or persons
to build
or operate tv and radio stations.
the telecommunications act of 1996
legalized monopolies.

Therefore,

the william s. paley family (CBS),
dictates what we eat, shit and sleep.
they control how we communicate,
what our kids lust,
work visas for illegitimate citizens
so you can have someone to hate.

edward j. noble and louis bamberger (ABC)
sling information on the infestation
of aids, sars, anthrax,
small-chicken-monkey pox.

jeff zucker (NBC) covered up
junior's political slip up
in big brother's backyard,
changing the union
while we changed the station.
and chester laroche (CNN)
broadcasted the 9-11's leveled
by bronzed skin brethren
who economically own
over 7% of your patriot-act-ass.

five chiefs serve universal dishes of propaganda
conditioning us to tune in, while tuning out
the travesties of children raped, battered and bruised.

they possess the power
to narrate a passion for war.
they glorify the tragedy
of a modern day marilyn monroe (anna nicole)
but bury the injustice of a 15 year old
imprisoned (for over a year) for pushing a teacher.

the disempowered pout about the power
they can't reclaim
while fake-ass Indian chiefs
swing tomahawks at our brains.

The King Center
(to Martin Luther King, Jr.)

A passion to follow a *dre*am
inspired me to follow my own,
crossing a busy West Main,
ascending Fairmount to a raised ranch
slightly extending that rocky cliff
behind the fire station.
A white signpost hailed your *legacy*
as I swung open a solid pine door.

In the far right corner of a large, single room
an abundance of snacks beckoned--
devoured and rinsed with frosty colas.
Elevated floorboards staged
Kung Fu Theater throwbacks.
Pardoned fourth graders sang to the mantra
of . . . *pencils* . . . *books* . . . and *dirty looks* . . . .
Salted kernels buttered in delight
wedged between my greasy fingertips
applauded an oversized lizard
wading through the Pacific
returning home in sheer victory.

I remember your *dream* . . . the nightmares,
the uncertainty of a solid pine door swinging
or jolting, sending shockwaves
up startled arms to broken hearts.
Closed. No center this summer.
Budget cuts forgot about us.
Lack of allocated funds,
a repetitive phrase we didn't understand
but understood as 1981, three, five and seven
produced rattled limbs and wounded spirits.
Over and over again politics denied our pardons
like ravenous children promised "happy meals."

Petersburg, VA

I boarded the morning train
squeezing mommy's coarse hand,
giggling at the Conductor's funny hat
propped on the top of his head.
The clank of metal against silver pathways
carried us across the Mason-Dixon
deeper into the South, leaving behind
a New England ocean breeze.
Boxcars swayed like an afternoon tide.
The whistling sound of steam
signaled our descent past Newport News.
Our voyage down the Eastern shoreline
was a summer tradition
for mommy, aunt Lois and me.
Except for the time when mommy
brought the twins; them nagging pests,
this was my get-a-away, my escape.
How could she?

We arrived in front
of a familiar beige house.
The wooden porch cracked
from Southern heat waves.
"Dallas," is what Mommy called him.
I knew him as "Granddad,"
his oily skin covered in wrinkles,
cracked frames
magnifying his yellowish eyes.
His thick, black hands,
strong as a lion's;
the first to course seedling
at Yantic Grain,
build submarines
at EB, taught Mommy
how to pivot, and strike

"South Paw" style,
before they were shipped
to Iowa Jima,
from whence they returned
but never back to the shores
of a New England breeze.

Sadee, his new wife,
fried catfish over a gas-stove.
The crackling grease unfurled
the scent of golden cornmeal
into the front room,
behind the coat rack,
where I would tear off my clothes
and remove Granddad's frames
to rescue a frantic *Lois Lane*
from a diabolical *Lex Luther*,
until dinner was ready.

On muggy nights,
I'd conceal my secret identity,
plop beneath the living room fan
and gaze at an orange,
Virginian moon
casting four-legged shadows
across a dusted floor.
My X-ray vision
exposing crumbs of cornmeal
carted into darkness.

Blanford Elementary
threw end of summer block parties,
grown-folk feeling the funk
as August steam rose from old souls
soaked in Rhythm & Blues.
Longing to be "grown,"
I'd get my "backyard boogie" on

from across the street,
jammin' on the front porch
to Whodini's *Five Minutes of Funk*,
with the countdown
steadily commencing . . .
One minute left . . . .

When the muggy nights began to cool
and a translucent moon
consumed the nocturnal sky,
I'd squeeze mommy's coarse hand,
pinpoint the North Star
and slowly ascend the Mason-Dixon
to the shores of a New England breeze.

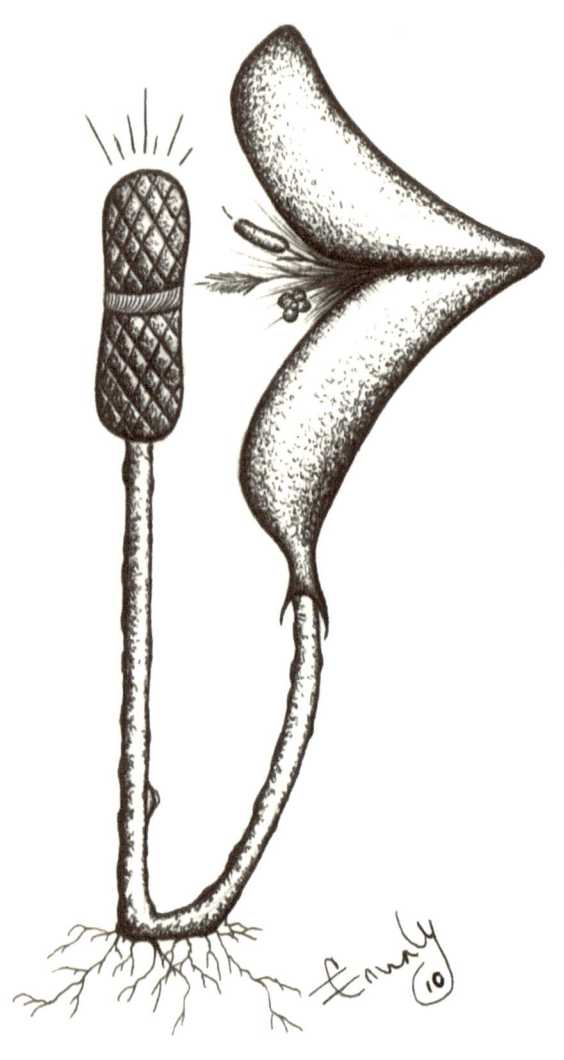

KICK THE CAN
(summer nights at "575")

The blaze of an august sun
melts into the nocturne.
Ripened crickets summon mates
to full moon fantasies.
Fireflies unveil hidden cracks
in shadows of the unknown
as a thick coat of blackness entices
silhouettes pressed
against the kitchen window.

When the sternness
of mommy's stature
submitted to our symphonies
of "can we please . . ."
we'd bolt down the stairs,
pile into the front yard,
form a circle and commence . . .
"1,2,3 not it!"

Raymond is the first relieved.
Round 2; exoneration soothes
the involuntary spasm
jolting down the backside
of my left leg.
Rounds 3, 4, 5 and 6
bubble gum,
bubble gum in the dish . . .
liberates the twins
while the neighborhood gang
(Danny, Elaina, Laura Porter and the Perkins)
follow suit. Jamie pleads best out of three.

An orange *Crush* plucked
from Gammy's refund stash,
a heap of "would-be" nickels
jumbled in a tattered plastic bag
concealed from *can-kicking culprits*
is placed in front of the porch steps.
Tag-a-longs are forewarned not to follow
as summer-night-cosmonauts
blast off into a pit of blackness.

Shrubs, posed as double agents
prevent sultry air from revealing secrecies
as we crept & crawled around backyard corners
lying dormant in thick blades of grass
like a creeping lioness stalking her prize.

A still figure dangles in the apple tree.
Another, angles between pear trees
and the path leading down
the backside of the far garage.
The grapevine swallowed by the abyss
is off limits.

The Cankeeper tactically executes his conquest.
The *Wrath of Khan* unleashed.
Midnight Marauders scurry into the open.
The twins are the first caught.
"Tap, tap, tap on Lee on the side of the garage!"
Lisa soon follows. The apple tree's cloak ineffective.
3,4,5 & 6 are caught to the rhythm of aluminum
clanking against concrete.

The welcoming wall
at Thames Valley Community College
symmetrically across the street,
enables marksmanship.
A silver cylinder gleams to humming streetlamps.

Slowly, I cross the quiet, glued to the fence,
rose thorns prickling my clammy flesh.

Jamie peers into darkness.
I rise. He turns.
Eyes locked.
He squints. Focuses.
--Spotted.   I dash.
Flawless strides.

His abrupt stumble
offers me the jump.
I size up the "C"
in the center of the can
like a kicker eyeing the snap
3 seconds left, down by 2.
I plant my foot, cock back my right,
his outstretched arm inches away
--WHAM!!!

Hollow metal hurls into darkness.
The imprison scatter into moonbeams.
The tatty cylinder repositioned.
The Cankeeper commences…
" 1 Mississippi, 2 Mississippi . . .
ready or not here I come!"

West Side

The burning sun
radiates off steamy concrete.
A pounding basketball
engenders ancestral bass lines
summoning full-court warriors to battle.
Crossover connoisseurs form tribal squadrons.

Rival leaders
select devoted combatants
 in search of conquest.
Salted sweat seeps from pores
wiped away by flushed hands.
A splash of cool water
revitalizes somnolent opponents
in mere points from claiming the throne.

Tony's matchstick legs didn't prevent him
from waddling down court
raining three's for 40 days and nights.
Lil' Charlie's small frame and sharp wit
enticed adversaries to test his wild left-hand style,
leaving competitors dumbfounded
as the sacred sphere breezed behind his back,
to his right, across the lane and off the board.
The rattling clank of metal
echoed throughout the park
as he smacked the rusted surface
with authority.

Somehow, Phil's unorthodox technique,
one hand on pants, the other on ball,
was sufficient enough for him to achieve victory,
releasing his grip just long enough

to sink a jumper in your face,
quickly re-capturing his belt-less denims
before they slid past his ankles.
> Amazing, how the drum line
> of the *Motherland*
> pulsed in each warrior, each riding
> Her rhythm to a sundry beat.

Jay-Gill could post up, push off,
lean back into a fade away
and back peddle down court
to the snapping sound of the net,
flashing his signature grin from ear to ear.
Boo, a legendary Zulu,
consistently stroked from half-court
before 3-point lines were ever fathomed.

Battle cries from antagonistic,
shit-talkin' "I got next-ers"
outlined the battlefield:
> E-Boone, Awol, Arty Clay,
> Bo-Ski, Shank, Dog,
> "Sweet Dick" Willie, Al, Ice, James,
> Lil' Henry, Butterball and Jerome
all declaring war against reigning victors.

Warriors, who never set foot
 in Saharan sand, were sent Home
through syncopated bounce passes.
Alley-hoops sent them sailing
like true descendants of flying Africans
> declaring freedom.

Big C.
(Illmatic '94)

I'd hit the repeat button
over and over
reciting track 3 line for line . . .

AZ's timeless chorus
rang to not so distant memories.
Olu Dara's incessant trumpet solo
consumed the smoke-filled air.
I'd close my eyes
and envision Big C's wide,
Caribbean-white smile,
baby-locks barely scrapping
his shoulder blades.
Reminiscing
like Pete Rock & CL Smooth,
I'd tap bottles and poured out liquor
paying hood homage.

Envisioning the realism of a lost life,
the native scent of Barbados
slid softly off his stories,
fallen comrades in worn fatigues
hustling in front of mosquito-infested tenements.
The soles of Timbs trudged blood-soaked furrows.
Hand-held cannons cracked the midnight sky.

Money mentality,
fearle$$ when we made it.
Recalling the first time
he watched me bag 20's.
His puzzled stare made me,

—a new-jack in da' game –
fumble half-folded lotto papers,
spilling cocaine into the cracks
of the kitchen floor.

He sailed from the core in search of a slice,
a piece of the golden, american't pie,
cinnamony-sweet, bitter to the bite,
brown eyes of a Brooklynite wide shut,
Canarse kept calling.
BlackRose kept'em *creaming*,
cut-throating competition
to the *snap-crackle-pops* of red tops.

His mocha hands exchanged pain
through palms of kinfolk
clutching vials of shattered vision.

We started on the block
 little $horties, pure hearts
but the fun & games stopped
when money became the plot
Climbing rank through Mechanic's backstreets,
Big C gaining respect
for tours of duty in the rotten core
          where *baseheads*
          inhale toxic vapors
          in rusted stairwells
          smothered in the stench of piss.
He made moves with the General,
          a veteran leader,
          waging troops out of a war
          against illicit pharmaceuticals
          peddled without licenses,
          titles of entitlement
          reserved for municipal agents
          probing *jacks*

out of black ass cracks,
injecting black phalluses
dangling from hips,
selling seizures back to blocks
to watch media-politic talk shit
on 5,6,7,10,11 o'clock news.

A purple heart pinned to a West Indin'
fervent of late night missions,
pushing adversaries 10 steps back
        violators of crack commandments
        prophesied by one of BK's finest.
He devised counter-attacks,
secretly disposed burning pieces
of smoke-filled blue steel.

Enemies sworn to
reppin' they block,
slingin' rock,
tottin' glocks
anticipated retaliation.
Their blood shot pupils soaked in rage
descended. Pistols pointed.
The breastplate of a soldier penetrated.
The vernal silence of an equinox
blossomed to the sound of hammers.

GREAT SKATE

They closed our Friday
"All-Nite" skating scene, so we
became drug-dealers.

Daddy's Little Girl

Frolicking underneath her Barney comforter,
she chuckles at the parade of Looney Tunes
caressing her powder blue walls.
The faint thump in the distance
startles her early morning fantasy.
The second one leaves her longing
for that *left turn at Albuquerque.*
The front door crashes.
Uniformed men storm upstairs
waving shiny black shooters.
They shout commands
in a language foreign to her soft ears.
Her father leaps from his bed,
met with six-shooters similar to Yosemite Sam's.
Get your ass on the ground! He obeys,
his bare chest pressed against the carpet.
Her mother's silent tears denote compliance.
Five years of life, *she* stands, frozen.
Her father hog tied.
Baby powder concealed
in a clear plastic bag, examined.
Young, ebony eyes plead for *Mommy.*
Disappointed.
Droplets of shame course his sullen cheeks.
Flashes of reddish-blue fade in the distance.
Men with five-star, shining pieces of silver,
pinned to chests, take her father away.

Rose City's Finest
(for Nia)

They found your body
Floating in the Thames River
And *gave not a fuck.*

LITTLE GREEN BOX

For Eve Montgomery Knowles:
December 31, 2001

my sweet little niece, Eve,
knowing nothing about you,
i have to write something.

i have to tell everyone
that i love you.
your family loves you.

here such a short period of time
leaving behind broken hearts,
leaving behind
a little green box,

a box containing
the elements of your existence,
containing a picture of an angel
with closed windows to her soul,

a little green box
containing a hat,
comb,
p.j.'s
and lock of hair.

Clouds

I.

powdered-soft mountains
floating --Godspeed
forming waves in unison
blanketing open space

II.

universal gatekeepers
moistened terrain
incapable of climbing;
of posting flags; claiming first rites

III.

silhouette of the Creator
as fine as She may be;
ascending Her powder-soft…. flirting
with the infinite possibilities of Her womb

IV.

conception , *Go Tell It On The Mountain*
gaze into Her wonderment
blanketing open space
floating --Godspeed.

Rose City Thorns

Toto,
I remember the way
you would tell me
to lie flat on my back,
as if positioned
for my very first sit-up.
You'd squeeze my tiny ankles,
ask if I was *ready*,
and catapult me into the air.
My tiny frame whirled
from a perfect release
into a full back flip,
a massive head-rush,
and I landed
squarely on my feet, giggling,
pleading for another,
then another, and another.

Rab,
you stood outside the back stoop
leaned against the rusted, metal post
and watched me lace up.
I felt the pressure, even though I knew
I could beat my opponent.
Still, my chest flamed.
I remember thinking
that if I won the backyard grudge,
I would gain the honor
of dating your daughter.
Now, nearly twenty years later,
I see you glancing at me
through my daughter's eyes.

Neicy,
you would call weed *fudama*.

You were the lone orator
of a dead discourse.
I remember how I would sell you poison,
and watch you and my brother
cook it, smoke it, and fiend for more.
I watched your youngest son,
barely eight, run back and forth
desperately seeking your attention
while the *strange man*
who only came around
twice a month
stole his lunch money
from your hand.

Who
could have comprehended your cries
and understood your fears
as the virus infiltrated?

Old friends, who believed
it only consumed
fags and *junkies,* misunderstood you.
They isolated you, pointed their fingers
when you walked down the street,
sat for a drink, attempting to drown
infectious T cells conquering your kingdom.
Those friends didn't know shit.
They couldn't have possibly
fathomed the casualties,
millions caught in the crossfire
of pharmaceutical warfare.

The absent-minded
who dodge the virus' bullet,
still whisper memories in the dark,
exchange theories
of who fucked you raw,

passed you that dirty needle
unleashing the *monster*
into the bedroom of your veins.

I don't feed your memories
with phantom stories
of the boogeyman,
gossiping secrets of contraction.
Your memories feed me,
giving me the strength
to fight this pathological war,
like ultraviolet sunlight
nurturing wilted rose petals
dwindling into a thicket of thorns.

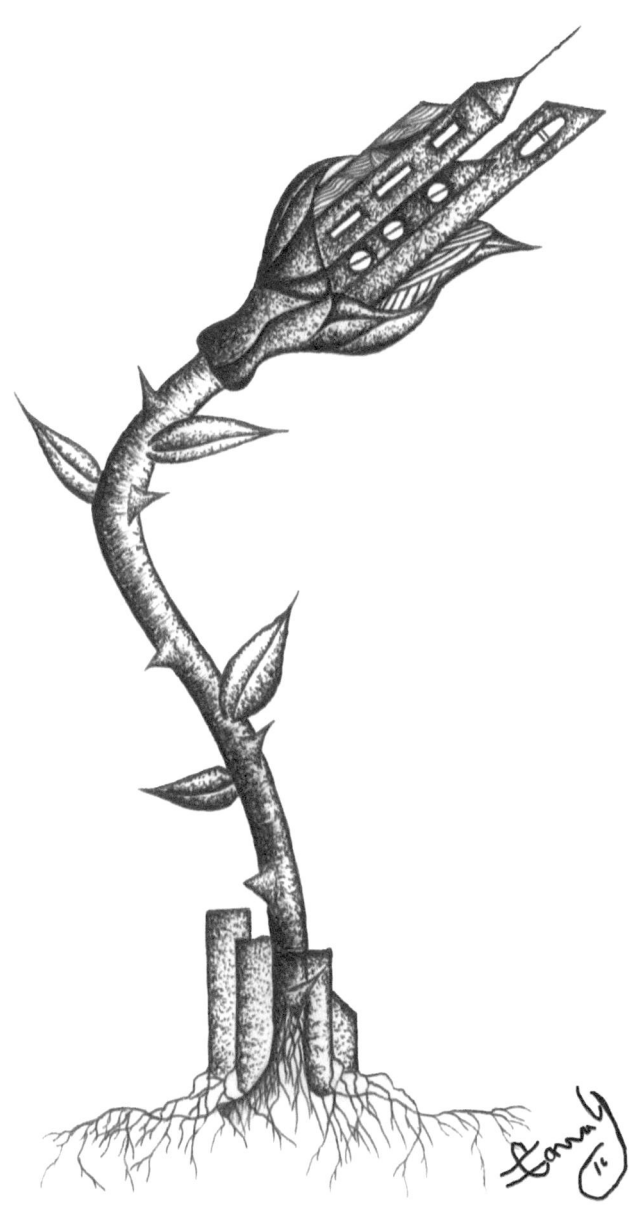

JamieForestKnowles

My brother's bright smile
never discloses the pain.
It never gives way
to the plight of AIDS
running rampant
through his blood stream.

His childlike grin demands
immediate gratification,
a consequence of dementia
eating away his logic.
His once masculine jowls
have given way
to an empty mouth,
toughen gums supported
 by sunken cheekbones
the result of molars,
canines and wisdom
--extracted.

My friend Ed,
who shares a similar smile, said
It helps prevent opportunistic diseases
from grabbing hold of the immune system.

I dread my family's call.
The sound of a little sister's voice
uttering, *There's no more smile.*
The granules of an hour glass
determined to fulfill their promise.
But promises are meant to be broken.

My brother fights with every breath.
       twice, on his death bed
             --he fought.
       when advised to make
       funeral arrangements
             --he fought.
       the pastor summoned
             --he fought.
He defied death,
softly gazed into its face
blew it a compassionate kiss
and walked away.

He lives.
He breathes.
He smiles.
He smokes,
       the only addiction
       he can't seem to shake.

Cigarettes and sex
numbed the innocence
of stolen adolescence.
Dime bags and *White Lines*
masked the memories
of molestation,
reluctantly *kissing cousins*
20 minutes in the closet,
open sores from extension cords
slicing his bound wrists, worn socks
absorbing his tears; gagging his cries.
Blood-torn tissue smothered in stool
made him walk a little lighter
hold his tongue a little less longer.

A timid smile deteriorated
 into a promiscuous leer.

No need for a closet,
he practiced with pride
and without protection.

Never no shame in his game.
There still isn't.
Patrons spanned from
tough guy to tinker bell,
gay to straight, family to friend.
And through it all,
he never denied the sullen stare
from the *man in the mirror*.
He never ignored
the cold smirk of his inner self,
quick to tell you to *go fuck yourself*
if he didn't fancy your type.
Hustlin' the streets
so the streets could hustle him,
his indecisive choice.
We accepted it.
Hell, we were doing it
–how could we not?

The formula was simple:
stay high & drunk
and fuck your worries away
and when the sun came up
repeat the past to ease the pain.

CHI-CHI HANK:

Private Raymond Keith Knowles Jr.

I gaze
into his graduation pic
grappling over lost time.
A stern figure
emits a soldier's glare.

His solid eyes pierce
the scoping lens.
Chiseled jowls crease
at 90°; no smile, focused.
His ancestral *LaNubian* heritage
resonates like Che
liberating the *Congolese*;
Zapata amalgamating
haciendas in *Morelos*.

A red-white-blue republic flag
crops a darkened background
foreshadowed
by his broad shoulder.
The legacy of a 4th generation,
Knowles
tatts the left side of his uniform;
his code of honor flanking the right.

Chi-Chi Hank ain't
little no more, baggy jeans
pulled to the waist side,
elongated white "T's"
tucked below the belt,
Nike "Air-Force One's"
marching to a stammering
commander in chief.
M-4 *lock and load*(ed).

Bullet-proof armor plates
deterring shraps of hot lead.
Grenade pouches
pack atomic blasts.
30 round magazines strapped.
He's 7 ½ lbs. stronger, deployed
in the land of mortars,
sand-dusted helmet fastened
no games on this field
--fourth and short--
human bombs
cloaked as children.

Chi-Chi Hank ain't
my *little* nephew no more,
laminated photo clutched
in the palm of my hand.
His spirit, still
like a freedom-fighter totting
BlackSteelintheHourofChaos,
praying that his devout faith
will keep the shepherd's flock
from the war-wolves
bloodthirsty for crude.

Rosemary's Babies
(Norwich's forgotten youth)

impoverished beads
starving like the Messiah
on the 41st

Canterbury Tale
(coming from Buddha's)

I lay in a stupor
squished in the backseat,
spiced rum coursing my veins.
Two more hits off the *haze*
fastened my eyelids.
O'Dog, in the front,
had been bumping the stereo.
Willie and "KP" conjured excuses
for not bagging any pussy
at the party. Violator
grasped the wheel
cutting corners like Andretti,
oblivious to the Oak
around the bend of a sharp curve.

The car lay on its side,
crushing Violator's arm
the stereo still bumping.
My skin was covered
in warm blood, gushing
from a head wound
embedded with glass.

Stuck between a stagger
of intoxication and inquietude,
I climbed out my window
and ran towards a dark driveway,
gravel crunching with desperation.
My trembling palms
soaked in the color of war
banged against a wall
of transparency.
My strained vocal cords
pled for *help*. No answer.

In the distance,
the crew shouted
for their lost mate
feared thrown overboard
at impact.

The midnight air crooned
ominous whispers
from a daunting tree line.
It's not our time. Not mine.
Fatherhood awaits tomorrow.

The doctor said,
Your face looks like a hamburger
a jargon tailored for a butcher:
His hands felt like meat cleavers
probing my raw flesh.
This isn't the morgue, there's light.
Mommy stood firm in her faith:
". . . here, Fred . . .
God wants you to stay here."

Through a cracked door
I heard a whimpering voice:
Freddy, my chest, I can't breathe.
I can't, breathe.
I never saw his face
but knew Willie was okay.
Uncertainty remained for the others.

The butcher's meat cleavers
pinned my mangled brow.
The cool needle pierced
my outer lid.
Numbness crept
down the side of my crease,

my waterline
overflowing with aqueous.
My lungs filled with caterwauls.
Grasping mommy's hand
 I lay full of conviction.
My eyelids no longer fastened.

Déjà Vu
(for Josh Sawyer)

I.

23
motionless
blood-pool
friends
ecstatic
pleading

II.

jagged steel
crackling glass
faint pulse
liquored fumes
nocturnal moonlit

III.

chest pumps
mouth to mouth
convulsions
involuntary reaction
Reaper awaiting

IV.

still moon
friends
flow rivers

V.

sirens
flashing lights
interrogation
orders
Get lost

VI.

dispersal
recollection
my latest
near death
experience
2 am, Route 2
eyes leaden
angel (Aunt Catherine) shouting
awakened
tailspin
Mack truck

VII.

the present
Samaritan
offers wipe
his blood stain
removed

VIII.

destination
home
headlights
beaming

IX.

revelation
2 am
phone call
mother
dreadful

X.

familiar scene
drinking
driving
13 years,
4 days prior;
2 days before
1st daughter's birth

Gallery Walls

(for Daddy Poncho)

> Stone masons have the right of the creator.
> They make bridges and churches, school steps and sculptures.
> They make mills out of stone and it is them that make gravel.
> They make chippings. By hand.
>
> —Lindsey Collen

I had no idea,
passing through sliding doors
cramming into a kitchen
where Ma stirred pots of *Cachupa*
'til grumblin' bellies simmered

 …no idea,
when I turned the corner
past the front room
where photogenic smiles
from the isles of African ancestry
coated post-colonial walls

no clue,
as I approached the TV room
your swollen feet bathed in Epsom,
one hand grasping the remote
the other, clutching cancer.

I was mooned,
before sun beams formed
pink morning clouds;
prelusive grass blades
shook dewdrops into mist,
that your pallid hands
piled bluestone
into perfection. Oblivious, I was
how you gazed at fieldstones

visualizing an opus.

I was unaware, that even
in your sickest moment
a stubborn Poncho would declare
I'm going to work tomorrow
running worksites
from your blue truck
clinging Briar Hill road.

I was injudicious,
until your purpose
adorned gallery walls.
Them walls spoke conviction,
on how *your* walls --stand
mightier than Jericho's
withstanding trumpet blasts
crumbling for no one;
paying homage to ancestors
who built *Colossals* to keep
the Portuguese astray.

I had no idea
how great of a man you were
until I saw you, *still*
--hard as granite.

The 80's
(for BlackRoseCity)

A bed of Roses
Every night we sleep in
Summers, we'll miss not.

Suede Pumas

Summer, I wipe
the morning cake from my eyes,
lather my chocolate skin,
and race out the door.
Like a cool cat-daddy caressing 125th St.
I slide across a quiet Manwarring,
my blue suede Pumas styled
in a fresh pair of fat laces.

August tar clings
to the bottom of my shoes.
Nuggets of gravel seep
into the crevice of my soles.
Dust clouds settle
where rubber and suede infuse.
In a single swipe,
I tactically remove the hindrance.
My fingertips soaked in saliva.

Decked in my latest *B-Boy* apparel,
I elude "Lilac Island"
--the thick, cluster of mauve
that enchants hazy afternoons,
recovering lost treasures,
forcing fickle shipmates
to walk the plank.
I instinctively maneuver
around the clotted terrain
-- hardly in the mood for piracy.

The wooden porch creaks.
I grasp Charlene and Linda's glass door,
shoving aside the front one,
leaving it wide open.

I ascend their narrow flight of stairs,
tap in secret code, and await
the "*oooh's*" and "*aaah's.*"

Your shoes are awesome!
Charlene shrieks. Linda,
peeps over her shoulder
to catch a glimpse.
I got'em last night.
I begged my mom for two days straight,
recalling the flame that set me ablaze
nearly three nights ago
when Charlene, Linda, Artie and I
scrunched in the *Palace Theatre* seats
and absorbed the swift
break dancing moves of *Beat Street*,
Lee's fresh pair of Puma's
flashing across the silver screen.

Linda caresses the white insignia
on the inner side of my left sole.
I, play it cool. *Charlene & Linda*
Breakfast, their mother reaffirms.
We exchange goodbyes with promises
to meet on the *side* of "Lilac Island."
I give the girls a final glimpse,
shoot down the stairs, ignore the handle
and press my hand clean through
the transparency. The shards of glass
slice my chocolate skin.

Numbness
oozes down the side of my face.
Burgundy droplets plunge
into a field of suede. *Uuggghhh!!*
I squawk in a language
only Charlie Brown could decipher.

The girls scream an octave higher.
They dash down the stairs,
grab my arms and scurry me
across a frantic Manwarring.
The August tar clings
To the bottom of my shoes.

A Family Letter:

To 575 New London Tpke.
Norwich, CT 06360

To my mother
Half-News (LaForest),
who can't keep a story straight
but earnestly
taught eleven lazy children
that her humble voice,
fresh from shouting *Hallelujah's*
at Friday night church service,
could flame at the sight
of a dirty kitchen
she made clear
was to be cleaned.

Two hours of praise
led the church van
to pull alongside the fence.
The van door slammed.
Her worn heels clattered up the stairs.
The doorknob creaked
and she turned the corner
with Bible in hand,
to a sink-full of plates
and a floor covered in crumbs.

She spoke in tongue.
The *Hallelujah's* transformed
into *You damn kids.*
Her fury released Armageddon,
crashing dishes into kitchen crevices,
smashing any last dreams
of Saturday morning bowls
filled with *Captain Crunch.*

To my eldest brother
Harry Truman (Harvey),
the former pimp politic
who schooled a thirsty young-blood
on the political principles
of *pushin'* in the Rose.

He rapped about
old school cats,
the last of the *Macs*
reminiscin' of hey days
filled with fast ass and cash,
an addictive lifestyle
that turned big-timers
into junkies,
smooth *poppa-stoppas*
who never stopped numbin' the pain
snifflin' *deferred dreams*
sendin' streams of regrets
past nasal passages
seeped into clotted throats.
Her-on runnin' like rivers
washin' away worries
in a single *drip.*

Señor Pèpe (Michael),
the cool cat daddy
who kept it movin' & groovin'
zoomin' down the pike in his Impala,
dipped in silky smooth suits, black
Stacey Adams illuminating each step,
his favorite *Kangol* tipped to the side
slouched over left brow, peppermint
chew stick protruding his hustlin' lips,
the best of *Pendergrass* on repeat.

Screeching to a halt,
he'd pop from behind the wheel,
roll up on me with that look
of adventure in his eyes
and initiate inquiries
for late night festivities,
"—what's up dawg?"

Joy (Martha),
my *Boy* crazed surrogate mother
who shifted her eyes long enough
for Cabbage Head's exodus.
I explored the mysterious petals of the Rose
on my lonesome.
The frivolous cracks in the concrete
coursed city streets like seared veins
pulsating summer heat.

I wandered up and down Main Street
mesmerized by crowded eyes
as I past the police station,
where when asked, *What's your name?*
I replied, *Old Man Wolmack.*

Wild Horse (Patty), the firecracker
who concluded family cookouts
with beer bottles overflowing the trash.
An abrasive attitude fueled
short fuse wanna be dude
who'd drop-kick competitors
with the quick fast.

I'd re-enact her pro-wrestling theatrics
on old mattresses, bouncing off
jutted springs like turnbuckles,
using worn pillows as contestants
who caught two in the chest,
sent hurling to the canvass short of breath.

The exhilaration
of her unpredictable bombshells
fulfilled rainy-stuck-in-the-house-days
with chuckles and grins, recalling
family and friends icing bruised chins.

To *Ned* (Kenny),
the brown bag
in the back seat sailor
who swigged pints of Johnnie Walker
       red or black
late night, stumbling up steps,
mumbling conspiracy theories
behind family feuds.

He'd get pissed when interrupted,
storm out for no apparent reason
back into *Black's* streets
swerving in his T-Bird
       red or black.
On good days he'd place me,
the underage little brother
behind the wheel of the red one,
giving instruction
on how to adjust the mirror,
brake corners and follow tail lights
after having one too many.

Bonie (Donie),
the toothpick tomboy
who brought her brother
to Fresh Fest.
I stood in awe, as I saw
my Hip Hop Heroes rockin' the mic.
Buffy, The Human Beat Box, beatboxin'
while the Fat Boys
subdued in prison blues
rhymed about the consequences
of being *In jail because ya failed.*

The wisdom of Whodini
emphasized the importance of *Friends,*
told us we were *lucky to have just, One Love*
and warned all hip-hop heads that
The freaks come out at night.

Run-DMC
swarmed on *Sucker MC's.*
The King of Rock
made sure all the fly girls
knew his initial:
D- for never dirty,
MC- for mostly clean.
Run posed rhetorical questions
captivating his audience,
Whoooo's hooouse!?
declaring the stadium his domain,
Ruuun's hooouse!
while Jam Master Jay
Cut the record down to the bone.

The 5'2 bundle
of work boots & dungarees
planted the seed of a B-Boy/ MC
who 30 years later

would rock the mic
and declare the stage
a non-residency
for parasitical MC's.

Percy (Jamie),
the wear whatever
I can get my hands on
fashion show
who paraded the streets of *BlackRose*
colored coded in plaid & pastels.
My shirts and shoes
were merely his accessories
seized at leisure.

My missing pair of spandex shorts
re-emerged after the meet
prancing through the backroom
strapped to Percy's pelvis.
He being older than me,
I did the only thing
a younger brother could do,
Mommy! I'm telling on you!

Goose (Ray-Ray),
the long neck #33 QB,
who on *Any Given Sunday*
snatched his black and white cleats,
mouth piece and little brother
allowing me to stomp
with the big dogs.

He and the crew would conjure
at Mahan School, divvy the teams
and debate sandlot rules.
The edge of the sidewalk & fire hydrant
were the forbidden zones guarded to the end.
A tattered paper cup marked the first down.

Second and short,
he'd line me up adjacent to him,
hand me the slippery pigskin
and throw me a big brother block.
Defenders dived into divots of soil
missing their minutia target
as I scooted passed the solid red marker
and took it home, 14-7.

To *Showtime* (Johnnie-Lee),
the ill rendition of Mclean & 'Trane,
blowin' Slave Songs into Spirituals
Spirituals into Blues, Blues into Jazz
Jazz into Rock n' Roll . . . .

He'd drip puddles of sweat
soakin' all night sets
clenchin' his brass sax
at Kenney's Pub in *The Beat*

Ben Biello
would bang the backbeat
like *Blakey,*
Dezron Douglas
strummin' like *Mingus*
in his *Money Jungle,*
Kelly Powers
playin' the Baby Grand
like the daughter of a *Duke*
and Showtime settin' chords a fly
like *Bird* noddin' off sleep
to a *Be-Bop* sky.

Goady (Verna-Lisa),
the converted feral 'fro
cheerleader
turned star receiver
who kept me,
a junior deacon
in stitches
whenever Sista So & So
caught *the Spirit.*

The timid little sister
who would bang the bongos
-off beat, while Easter exhibitionists
rejoiced to her 1,2,1,1 syncopation.
Arms flailed. Skirts flapped
to her arrhythmic *tat, boom, tat, tat.*

Her old soul
is solid
like Sojourner's,
invincible
like Ida's,
harmonious
like Harriet's
totting *Bible* in one hand,
Rifle in the other.

To *Slumry* (Gammy),
the bet it all ex-bingo bookie
who flipped Sunday flapjacks
before Reverend Luther's van
transported her saints
to Sunday school.

My late night companion
who couldn't tolerate
a scared of the boogey-man grandson
wetting her bed. When she felt
the dampness of her sheets
she'd climb from under the covers
slide into her slippers
crack her bedroom door
and holler up the stairs,
Laforest, come get Fred!

Time and time again
she would say,
You're getting to old
to be sleeping with me
            and asked,
-What will your friends say
when you're in college?
I simply replied,
I won't tell'em.

To 575:
the foundation that raised
a lazy, inexperienced,
junior deacon,
pro-wrestling,
underage driving,
frightened football playing,
cabbage head looking,
bed wetting,
young blood
into a messenger
destined to spread luv & light.

Ashe.

No More Secrets

I told no one,
congealed lips
afraid to acknowledge
the jagged tears
coursing your cheeks
your tomboy tits
smeared in his stench
eternal nightmares
carved into your thighs
your cries, muffled intonations
on how he *came* with no consent.

We bolted out the backdoor
in pursuit of adolescent endeavors
your blouse unscathed,
cinnamon brown eyes
full of flare,
the two of you
lounging on the loveseat
tokin' *Newports*
drowning privation
in red rivers of *Wild Irish Rose.*

The Universe
sent me back.
Not your son.

I stood frozen
unraveling anguish
encrypted in confusion
your blouse torn
eyes full of despair
abandoned,
no one to pass
the last sip of privation

swirling
like your sanity
in the bottom of a bottle.

I left you,
said nothing
diverted my eyes
when your son passed the 40
drowning my privation
in the bottom of a bottle.

I knew wrong
but as children
we were taught
not to talk about *That*.

Except, we were
no longer children;
not quite old enough
to stumble into
high school dances
but old enough
to toke *Newports*
& swig pints of *Wild Irish Rose*
fantasizing about fucking
fast girls with big titties
frightened little boys –guised
scared the boogeyman
might come pay us a visit.

I remained silent
like the monster
who crept out of your closet,
defiled your *dreams*
and slid out the backdoor.

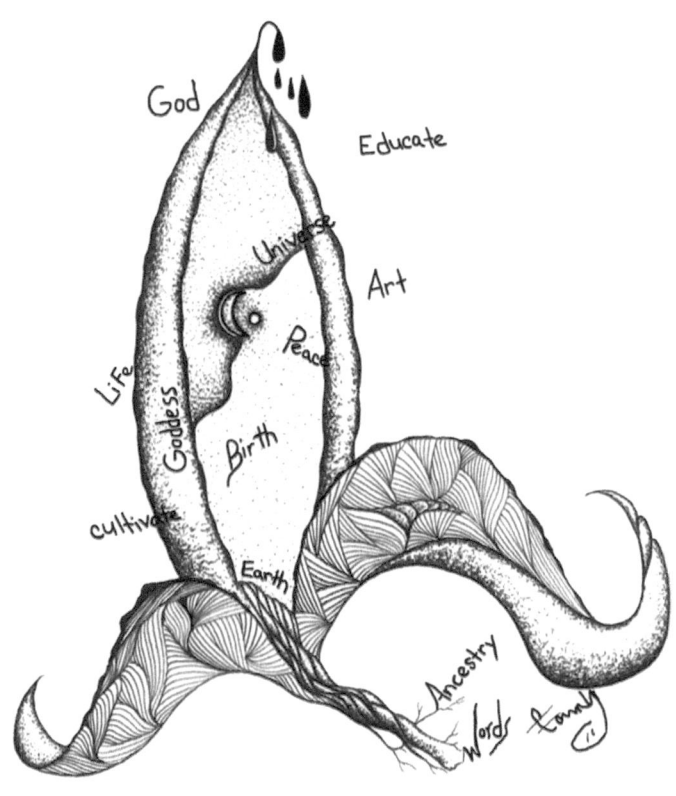

God

Educate

Universe

Art

Life

Peace

Goddess

Birth

cultivate

Earth

Ancestry

Words

76